If you liked this book, don't forget to leave a comment and a note on amazon.

This is really important for us.

A suggestion or a request?
thekarmafive@gmail.com

WHITE LADY

INGREDIENTS

- 2 ounces gin
- 1/2 ounce orange liqueur or triple sec
- 1/2 ounce lemon juice, freshly squeezed
- 1 egg white

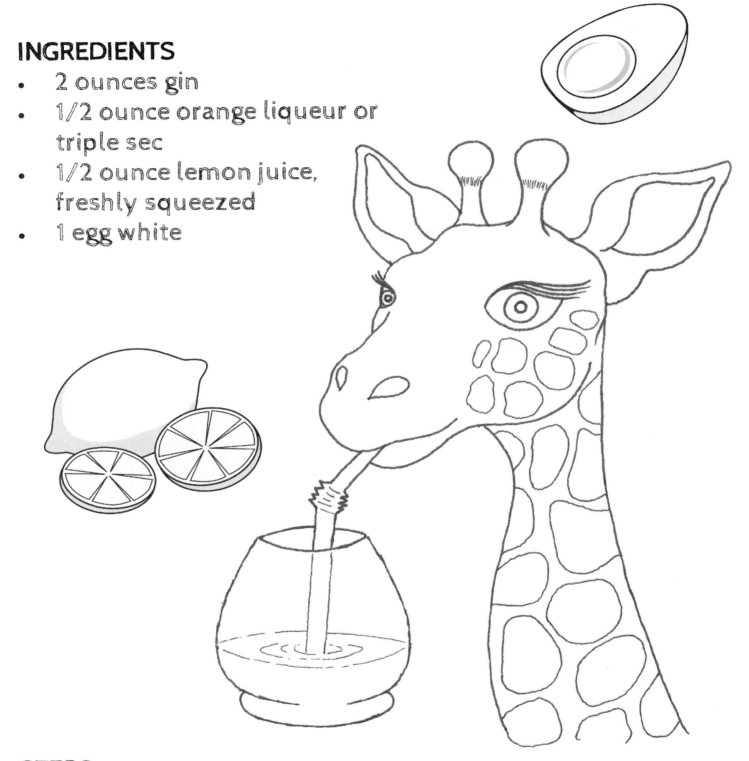

STEPS

- Add all ingredients into a shaker with ice and shake.
- Strain into a chilled cocktail glass.

BLOODY MARY

INGREDIENTS

- 1 lemon wedge
- 1 lime wedge
- 2 ounces vodka
- 4 ounces tomato juice
- 2 dashes Tabasco sauce
- 2 tsp prepared horse-radish
- 2 dashes worces-tershire sauce
- 1 pinch celery salt
- 1 pinch ground black pepper
- 1 pinch smoked pa-prika
- Garnish: lime wedge, green olives, parsley sprig, celery stalk

STEPS

- Pour some celery salt onto a small plate.
- Rub the juicy side of the lemon or lime wedge along the lip of a pint glass.
- Roll the outer edge of the glass in celery salt until fully coated.
- Fill with ice and set aside.
- Squeeze the lemon and lime wedges into a shaker and drop them in.
- Add the remaining ingredients and ice and shake gently.
- Strain into the prepared glass.
- Garnish with a parsley sprig, 2 speared green olives and a lime wedge and a celery stalk (optional).

TEQUILA SUNRISE

INGREDIENTS

- 2 ounces blanco tequila
- 4 ounces orange juice, freshly squeezed
- 1/4 ounce grenadine
- Garnish: orange slice
- Garnish: cherry

STEPS

- Add the tequila and then the orange juice to a chilled highball glass filled with ice.
- Top with the grenadine, which will sink to the bottom of the glass, creating a layered effect.
- Garnish with an orange slice and a cherry.

BOURBON OLD FASHIONED

INGREDIENTS

- 1/2 teaspoon sugar
- 3 dashes Angostura bitters
- 1 teaspoon water
- 2 ounces bourbon
- Garnish: orange peel

STEPS

- Add the sugar, bitters and water into a rocks glass, and stir until sugar is nearly dissolved.
- Fill the glass with large ice cubes, add the bourbon, and gently stir to combine.
- Express the oil of an orange peel over the glass, then drop in.

COSMOPOLITAN

INGREDIENTS
- 1 1/2 oz Citrus vodka
- 1 oz Cointreau
- 1/2 oz Fresh lime juice
- 1 dash Cranberry juice
- Garnish: Lime wheel

STEPS
- Add all ingredients into a shaker with ice and shake.
- Strain into a chilled cocktail glass.
- Garnish with a lime wheel.

DIRTY MARTINI

INGREDIENTS
- 2 1/2 ounces gin or vodka
- 1/2 ounce dry vermouth
- 1/2 ounce olive brine
- Garnish: 2 to 4 olives

STEPS
- Add all the ingredients into a mixing glass with ice and stir.
- Strain into a chilled cocktail glass.
- Garnish with 2 to 4 olives, skewered.

DAIQUIRI

INGREDIENTS

- 2 ounces light rum
- 1 ounce fresh lime juice
- 3/4 ounce demerara sugar syrup
- Garnish: lime twist

STEPS

- Add all the ingredients into a shaker with ice, and shake until well-chilled.
- Strain into a chilled coupe.
- Garnish with a lime twist.

MARGARITA

INGREDIENTS

- 2 oz Blanco tequila
- 1 oz Fresh lime juice
- 1/2 oz Orange liqueur
- 1/2 oz Agave syrup
- Garnish: Lime wheel, Kosher salt

STEPS

- Add all the ingredients into a shaker with ice, and shake until chilled.
- Strain into the prepared rocks glass over fresh ice.
- Garnish with a lime wheel and kosher salt (optional).

MOJITO

INGREDIENTS

- 3 mint leaves
- 2 ounces white rum
- 3/4 ounce fresh lime juice
- 1/2 ounce simple syrup
- club soda, to top
- Garnish: mint sprig
- Garnish: lime wheel

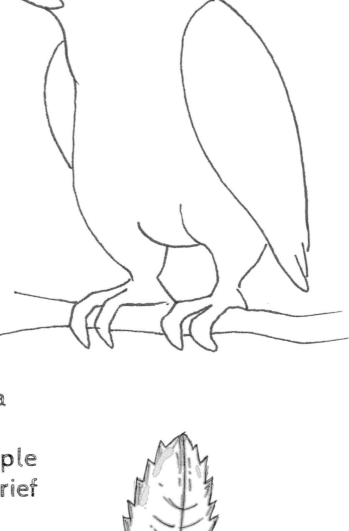

STEPS

- Lightly muddle the mint in a shaker.
- Add the rum, lime juice, simple syrup and ice and give it a brief shake.
- Strain into a highball glass over fresh ice.
- Top with the club soda.
- Garnish with a mint sprig and lime wheel.

PINA COLADA

INGREDIENTS

- 2 ounces light rum
- 1 1/2 ounces cream of coconut
- 1 1/2 ounces pineapple juice
- 1/2 ounce lime juice, freshly squeezed
- Garnish: pineapple wedge, pineapple leaf

STEPS

- Add all ingredients into a shaker with ice and shake vigorously (20-30 seconds).
- Strain into a chilled Hurricane glass over pebble ice.
- Garnish with a pineapple wedge and pineapple leaf.

SIDECAR

INGREDIENTS

- 1 1/2 ounce cognac
- 3/4 ounce orange liqueur (Cointreau or Grand Marnier)
- 3/4 ounce lemon juice, freshly squeezed
- Garnish: orange twist, sugar rim (optional)

STEPS

- Coat the rim of a coupe glass with sugar, if desired, and set aside.
- Add all ingredients into a shaker with ice and shake.
- Strain into the prepared glass.
- Garnish with an orange twist.

MANHATTAN

INGREDIENTS

- 2 ounces bourbon or rye
- 1 ounce sweet vermouth
- 2 dashes Angostura bitters
- 1 dash orange bitters
- Garnish: brandied cherry

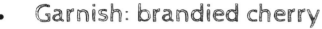

STEPS

- Add all the ingredients into a mixing glass with ice, and stir until well-chilled.
- Strain into a chilled coupe.
- Garnish with a brandied cherry.

BEET ROSE

INGREDIENTS

- 2 ounces Ketel One vodka
- 1 ounce fresh beet juice
- 3/4 ounce fresh lemon juice
- 6 mint leaves
- prosecco, chilled, to top
- Garnish: mint sprig, lemon twist

STEPS

- Add all ingredients except prosecco into a shaker with ice and shake until well-chilled.
- Double-strain into a highball glass over fresh ice.
- Top with prosecco.
- Garnish with a mint sprig and lemon twist.

RUM PUNCH

INGREDIENTS

- 1 1/4 ounces light rum
- 1 1/4 ounces dark rum
- 2 ounces pineapple juice
- 1 ounce orange juice, freshly squeezed
- 1/4 ounce lime juice, freshly squeezed
- 1/4 ounce grenadine
- Garnish: maraschino or brandied cherry

STEPS

- Add all ingredients into a shaker with ice and shake until well-chilled.
- Strain into a Hurricane glass over fresh ice.
- Garnish with a maraschino or brandied cherry.

PINK LADY

INGREDIENTS

- 6 ounces Hawkes Doom & Bloom Rosé Cider (or other rosé cider)
- 2-3 ounces cranberry juice
- 1 splash orange juice

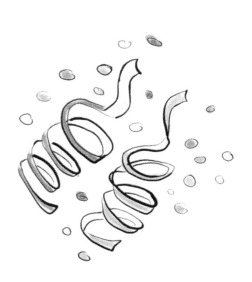

STEPS

- Add the cider into a pint glass.
- Top with the cranberry and orange juices and stir gently.

SPICED APPLE FIZZ

INGREDIENTS

- 1 1/2 oz ZU Bison Grass Vodka
- 1/2 oz Poire Williams Pear Brandy
- 1/2 oz Lemon juice
- 1/2 oz Honey syrup
- Hard apple cider
- Fresh grated cinnamon
- Garnish: apple slice fan

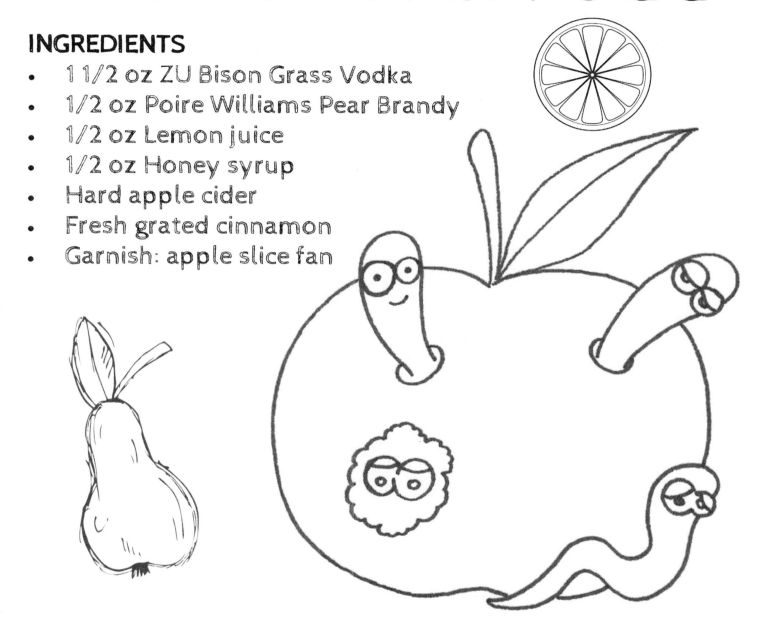

STEPS

- Add all ingredients (except the cider) to a mixing glass and fill with ice.
- Shake, and strain into a highball glass over fresh ice.
- Top with hard apple cider and garnish with an apple fan and fresh grated cinnamon.

BRAZILIAN BUCK

INGREDIENTS

- 1 1/2 ounces Novo Fogo Chameleon cachaça
- 4 ounces ginger beer
- 1 squeeze fresh lime
- 2 dashes aromatic bitters
- Garnish: lime slice, ginger peel

STEPS

- Add all ingredients into a highball glass over ice and stir to combine.
- Garnish with a lime slice and ginger peel.
- Serve with a straw.

KILLER QUEEN

INGREDIENTS

- 2 ounces aromatic gin
- 3/4 ounce dried-rose-infused Lillet Blanc
- 1/4 ounce Benedictine
- 4 dashes Angostura bitters
- Garnish: lemon twist

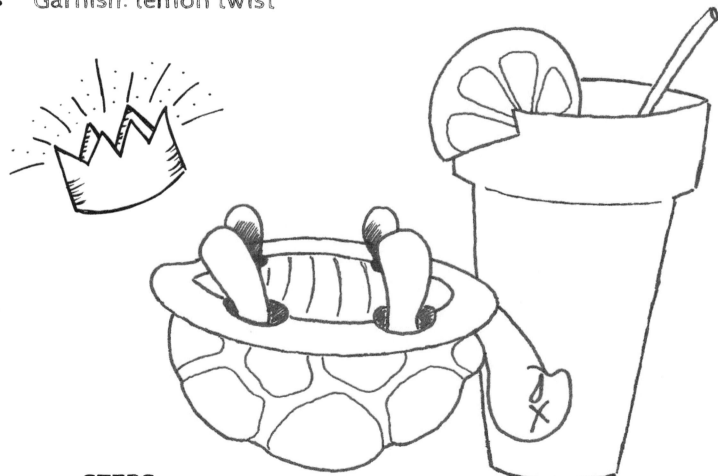

STEPS

- Add all ingredients into a mixing glass with ice and stir.
- Strain into a coupe.
- Express the oil from a lemon peel over the drink.
- Garnish with a lemon twist made from the peel.

KAMIKAZE

INGREDIENTS

- 2 oz Vodka
- 3/4 oz Orange liqueur
- 3/4 oz Fresh lime juice

STEPS

- *Makes 2 shots.*
- Add all the ingredients into a shaker with ice, and shake thoroughly until well-chilled.
- Strain into two shot glasses.

BLUE HAWAII

INGREDIENTS

- 3/4 ounce vodka
- 3/4 ounce light rum
- 1/2 ounce blue curaçao
- 3 ounces pineapple juice
- 1 ounce sweet-and-sour mix
- Garnish: pineapple wedge, cocktail umbrella

STEPS

- Add all ingredients into a shaker with ice and shake until well-chilled. (Or blend all ingredients with ice in a blender.).
- Strain into a Hurricane glass over crushed or pebble ice. (Or pour from blender into glass with no ice.).
- Garnish with a pineapple wedge and cocktail umbrella.

GIN FIZZ

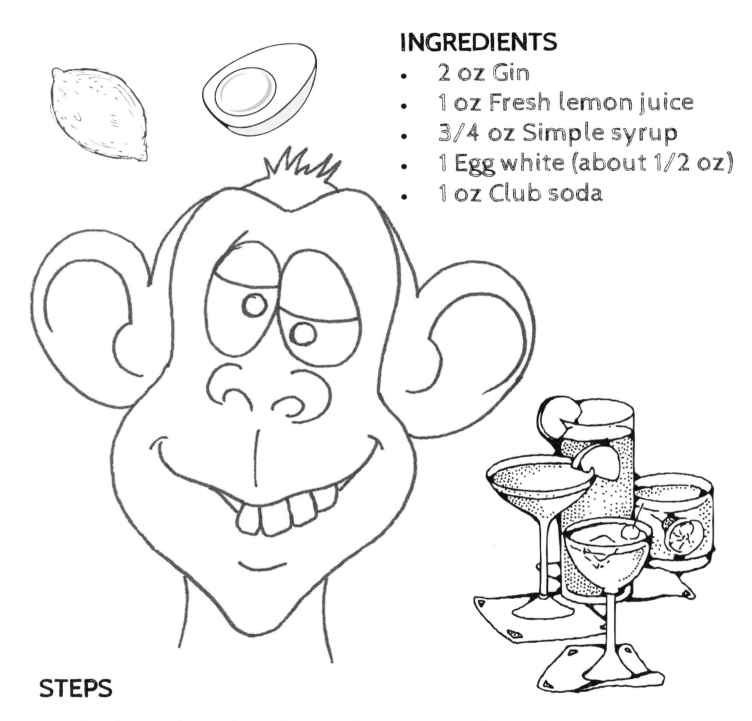

INGREDIENTS

- 2 oz Gin
- 1 oz Fresh lemon juice
- 3/4 oz Simple syrup
- 1 Egg white (about 1/2 oz)
- 1 oz Club soda

STEPS

- Add the first four ingredients to a shaker and dry-shake (without ice) for about 10 seconds.
- Add 3 or 4 ice cubes and shake very well.
- Double-strain into a chilled fizz glass and top with club soda.

HORN OF THE BULL

INGREDIENTS

- 1 1/2 ounce El Jimador blanco tequila
- 1/2 ounce Midori
- 1/2 ounce cucumber syrup
- 3/4 ounce pineapple juice
- 3/4 ounce heavy cream
- 1 egg white
- 1 pinch salt
- chilled soda water, to top
- Garnish: lime wheel

STEPS

- Add all ingredients except soda water into a shaker and dry-shake (no ice) to emulsify.
- Add ice and shake again until well-chilled.
- Double-strain into a Collins glass without ice and top with soda water.
- Garnish with a dehydrated or fresh lime wheel.
- *Cucumber syrup: Add 1/2 cup sugar and 1/2 cup water into small saucepan and cook on medium heat until sugar is dissolved. Remove mixture from heat, let cool slightly, then add 6 peeled slices of cucumber (1/2-inch-thick each). Allow to steep for 10 minutes, remove solids and store in refrigerator for up to a week.

LONG ISLAND ICED TEA

INGREDIENTS

- 3/4 oz Vodka
- 3/4 oz White rum
- 3/4 oz Silver tequila
- 3/4 oz Gin
- 3/4 oz Triple sec
- 3/4 oz Simple syrup
- 3/4 oz Fresh lemon juice
- Cola, to top
- Garnish: Lemon wedge

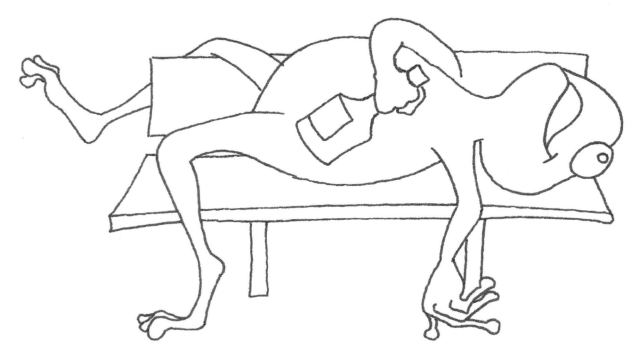

STEPS

- Add all ingredients except the cola into a Collins glass with ice.
- Top with a splash of the cola and stir briefly.
- Garnish with a lemon wedge.
- Serve with a straw.

GINGER FEVER PUNCH

INGREDIENTS

- 1 1/2 oz Blanco tequila
- 3/4 oz Fresh lime juice
- 3/4 oz Pomegranate juice
- 1/2 oz Grapefruit juice
- 1/2 oz Goji ginger syrup
- Fever-Tree ginger beer, to top
- Garnish: Pomegranate seeds, Sliced grapefruit, Rosemary sprig

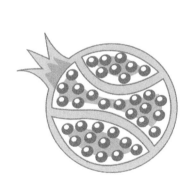

STEPS

- Add all ingredients except ginger beer into a shaker with ice and shake.
- Strain into a rocks glass over fresh ice.
- Top with ginger beer.
- Garnish with pomegranate seeds, sliced grapefruit and a rosemary sprig.
- *Goji ginger syrup: Add 4 oz ginger juice, 1/2 cups granulated sugar, 1 tbsp goji berries into a blender and blend at medium speed. Strain and pour into a sealed container. Keep refrigerated up to 2 weeks.

CHAMPAGNE COCKTAIL

INGREDIENTS

- 10mL cognac
- 15mL sugar syrup
- 2 dashes of bitters
- Orange slice, to garnish
- Maraschino cherry, to garnish

STEPS

- Pour cognac, sugar syrup, bitters, and Champagne into a Champagne flute.
- Garnish with an orange slice and a maraschino cherry.

TOM COLLINS

INGREDIENTS

- 2 Oz gin
- 3/4 Oz lemon juice
- 1/2 Oz sugar syrup
- Soda water, to top
- Lemon wedge, to garnish
- Maraschino cherry, to garnish
- Ice

STEPS

- Add gin, lemon juice and sugar syrup to an ice-filled cocktail shaker
- Shake well to blend
- Strain into an ice-filled Collins (or Highball) glass
- Top with soda water
- Garnish with a maraschino cherry and a lemon wedge

MAI TAI

INGREDIENTS

- 3/4 Oz white rum
- 3/4 Oz dark rum
- 1 Oz lime juice
- 3/4 Oz orange curacao
- 1/2 Oz orgeat syrup
- Pineapple wedge, to garnish
- Maraschino cherries, to garnish

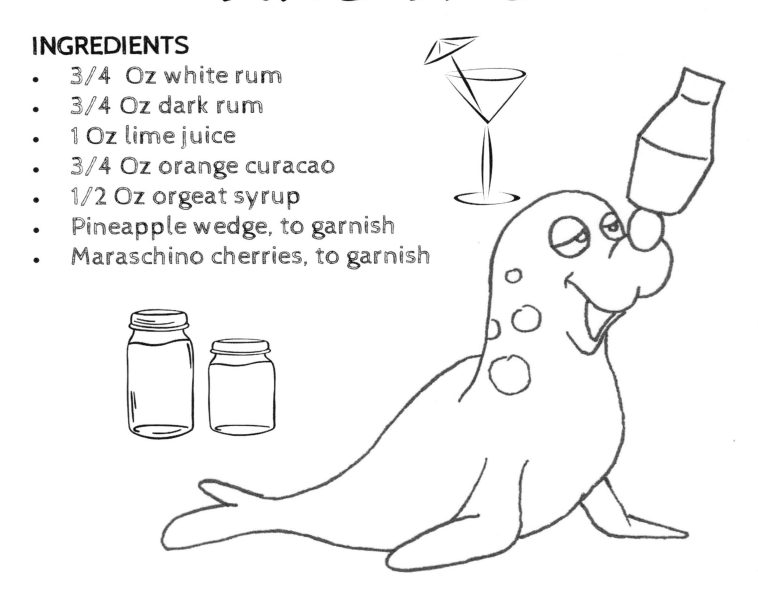

STEPS

- Add rum, orange curacao, orgeat syrup, lime juice, and ice to a cocktail shaker.
- Shake to blend.
- Fill a tall glass with ice.
- Strain drink into glass.
- Garnish with a maraschino cherry and pineapple wedge.

WHITE RUSSIAN

INGREDIENTS
- 1 Oz vodka
- 1 Oz coffee liqueur
- 1 Oz cream

STEPS

- Fill short glass with ice.
- Add vodka, coffee liqueur, cream, and stir.

LA DOLCE VITA

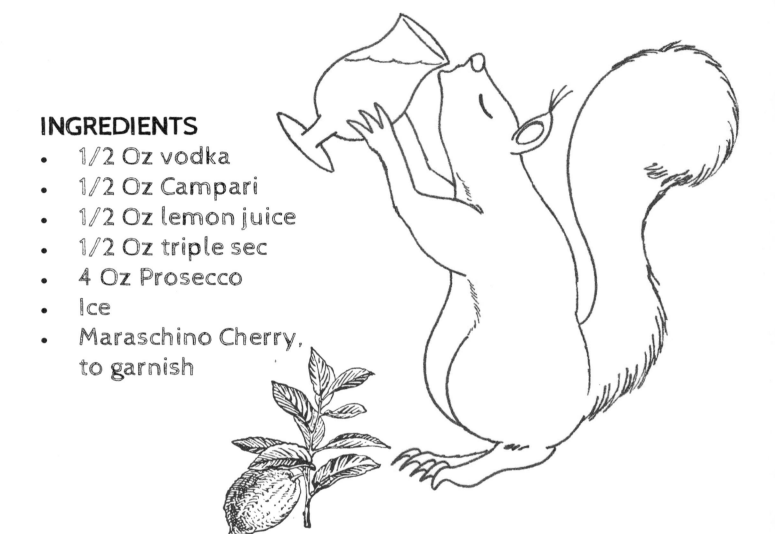

INGREDIENTS

- 1/2 Oz vodka
- 1/2 Oz Campari
- 1/2 Oz lemon juice
- 1/2 Oz triple sec
- 4 Oz Prosecco
- Ice
- Maraschino Cherry, to garnish

STEPS

- Add all ingredients except prosecco to a ice-filled wine glass.
- Stir well, top with prosecco and garnish with a maraschino cherry.

EL DIABLO

INGREDIENTS

- 1 1/2 Oz tequila
- 1/2 Oz creme de cassis
- 1/2 Oz lime juice
- 1/3 Oz sugar syrup
- Ginger ale, to top
- Lime, to garnish

STEPS

- Add tequila, creme de cassis, lime juice, sugar syrup, and ice to a cocktail shaker.
- Shake to blend, and strain into an ice-filled tall glass.
- Garnish with lime.

GRASSHOPPER

INGREDIENTS

- 1 Oz cream
- 1 Oz creme de menthe
- 1 Oz creme de cacao
- Chocolate sauce
- Mint leaves, to garnish
- Ice

STEPS

- Add cream, creme de cacao, creme de menthe, and ice to a cocktail shaker.
- Shake to blend.
- Swirl chocolate sauce around the inside of a martini glass.
- Strain cocktail into martini glass.
- Garnish with mint leaves.

BAMBOO

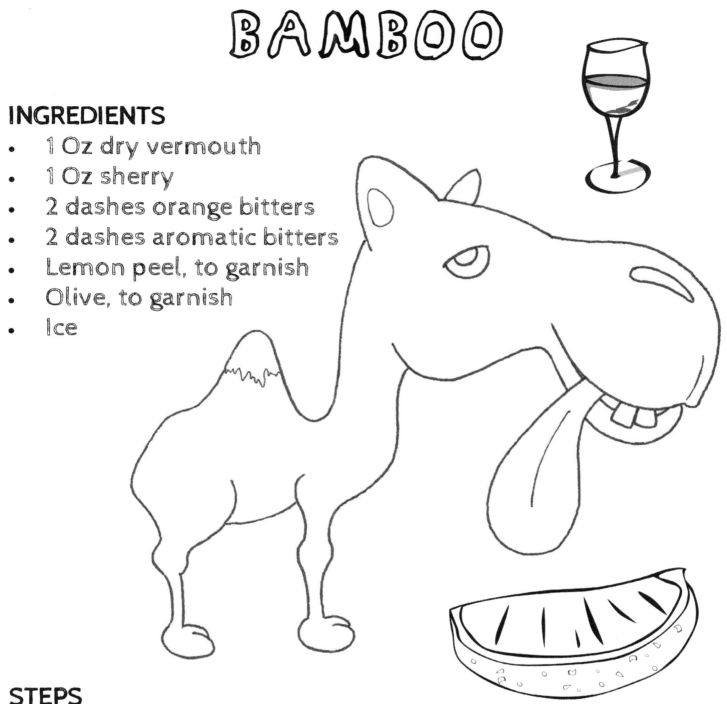

INGREDIENTS

- 1 Oz dry vermouth
- 1 Oz sherry
- 2 dashes orange bitters
- 2 dashes aromatic bitters
- Lemon peel, to garnish
- Olive, to garnish
- Ice

STEPS

- Add ice, bitters, dry vermouth, and sherry to a tall glass and stir.
- Strain into a martini glass.
- Spray lemon oil from lemon peel into martini glass.
- Garnish with lemon peel and olive.

AMERICANO

INGREDIENTS

- 1 Oz Campari
- 1 Oz sweet vermouth
- Soda water, to top
- Orange wedge, to garnish

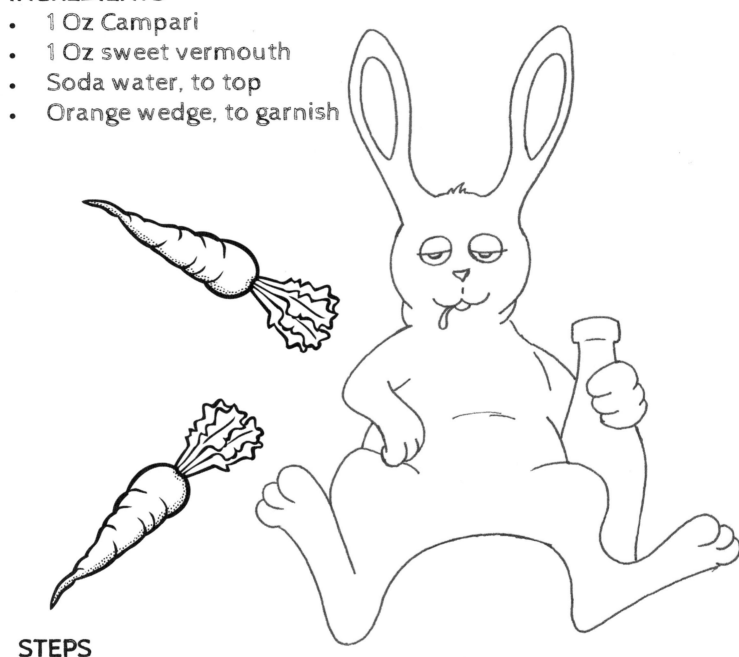

STEPS

- Add ice to a short glass.
- Add campari and sweet vermouth to short ice-filled glass.
- Top with soda water.
- Garnish with an orange wedge.

PALOMA

INGREDIENTS

- 1 1/2 Oz tequila
- 1/2 Oz lime juice
- Sparkling pink grapefruit, to top
- Grapefruit slice, to garnish
- Coarse salt, for the rim
- Lime juice, for the rim
- Ice

STEPS

- Run the lime on the rim of the glass then dip it in the salt.
- Fill the glass with ice, and add tequila and lime juice.
- Top with grapefruit juice.
- Garnish with grapefruit.

ROSITA

INGREDIENTS

- 1/2 Oz rosso vermouth
- 1/2 Oz dry vermouth
- 1/2 Oz Campari
- 1 dash bitters
- Lemon twist, to garnish
- Ice

STEPS

- Fill an Old Fashioned glass with crushed ice.
- Add all ingredients, and stir to combine.
- Garnish with a twist of lemon.

TREACLE

INGREDIENTS

- 2 Oz dark rum
- 1/3 Oz sugar syrup
- 2/3 Oz apple juice
- 2 dashes bitters
- Apple slice, to garnish
- Ice

STEPS

- Fill a short glass with ice.
- Add dark rum, sugar syrup, bitter to the glass and stir.
- Garnish with apple slices.

ANEJO HIGHBALL

INGREDIENTS

- 1 1/2 Oz aged rum
- 2/3 Oz triple sec
- 2/3 Oz lime juice
- 1 dash of bitters
- ginger beer, to top
- Ice

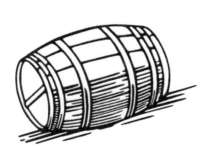

STEPS

- Add the rum, triple sec, lime juice and bitters to an ice-filled high-ball glass.
- Top with ginger beer and stir to combine.
- Garnish with mint.

FRENCH 85

INGREDIENTS

- 1 Oz American whiskey
- 1/2 Oz lemon juice
- 1/2 Oz sugar syrup
- 3 Oz Champagne
- Lemon twist, to garnish
- Ice

STEPS

- Fill a cocktail shaker with ice cubes.
- Add whisky, lemon juice and sugar syrup and shake well.
- Strain into a chilled Champagne flute.
- Top with Champagne and garnish with a lemon twist.

PARASOL

INGREDIENTS

- 1 Oz strawberry puree
- Prosecco, to top
- Strawberry, to garnish
- Ice

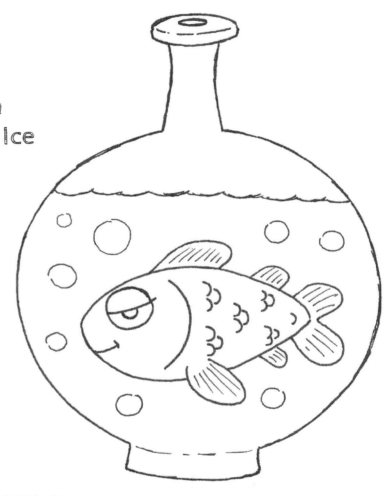

STEPS

- Add strawberry puree to a Champagne flute.
- Top with prosecco.
- Garnish with a slice of strawberry.

MIMOSA

INGREDIENTS

- 1/2 Oz triple sec
- 1 1/2 Oz orange juice
- 3 Oz Champagne or sparkling wine, chilled
- Orange slice, to garnish

STEPS

- Add triple sec and orange juice to a champagne flute.
- Top with sparkling wine.
- Garnish with a slice of orange.

NEGRONI

INGREDIENTS

- 1 ounce gin
- 1 ounce Campari
- 1 ounce sweet vermouth
- Garnish: orange peel

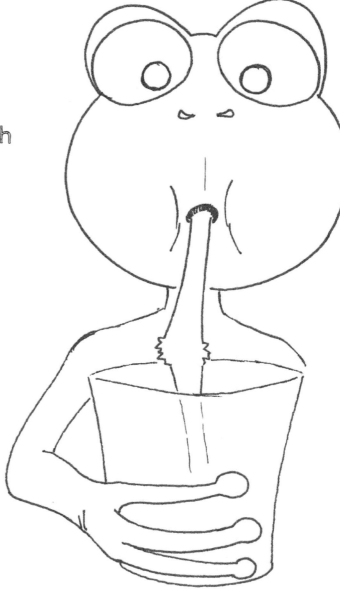

STEPS

- Add all the ingredients into a mixing glass with ice, and stir until well-chilled.
- Strain into a rocks glass filled with large ice cubes.
- Garnish with an orange peel.

ADONIS

INGREDIENTS

- 1 1/2 Oz fino sherry
- 1 1/2 Oz rosso vermouth
- 1 dash of orange bitters
- Orange twist, to garnish

STEPS

- Add all ingredients (except the orange twist) to a mixing glass and stir.
- Strain into a chilled cocktail glass.
- Garnish with orange twist.

HANKY PANKY

INGREDIENTS

- 1 1/2 Oz gin
- 1 1/2 Oz sweet vermouth
- 1/6 Oz Fernet-Branca
- Orange twist, to garnish
- Ice

STEPS

- Add gin, sweet vermouth, Fernet-Branca, and ice to a tall glass.
- Stir to combine, and strain into a Martini glass.
- Garnish with an orange twist.

And now YOUR own RECIPES

INGREDIENTS

- ....
- ....
- ....
- ....
- ....
- ....
- ....
- ....
- ....

STEPS

- ....
- ....
- ....
- ....
- ....
- ....

INGREDIENTS

- ....
- ....
- ....
- ....
- ....
- ....
- ....
- ....
- ....

STEPS

- ....
- ....
- ....
- ....
- ....
- ....

....

INGREDIENTS

- ....
- ....
- ....
- ....
- ....
- ....
- ....
- ....
- ....

STEPS

- ....
- ....
- ....
- ....
- ....
- ....

....

INGREDIENTS

- ....
- ....
- ....
- ....
- ....
- ....
- ....
- ....
- ....

STEPS

- ....
- ....
- ....
- ....
- ....
- ....

....

INGREDIENTS

- ....
- ....
- ....
- ....
- ....
- ....
- ....
- ....
- ....

STEPS

- ....
- ....
- ....
- ....
- ....
- ....

INGREDIENTS

- ....
- ....
- ....
- ....
- ....
- ....
- ....
- ....
- ....

STEPS

- ....
- ....
- ....
- ....
- ....
- ....

INGREDIENTS

- ....
- ....
- ....
- ....
- ....
- ....
- ....
- ....
- ....

STEPS

- ....
- ....
- ....
- ....
- ....
- ....

....

INGREDIENTS

- ....
- ....
- ....
- ....
- ....
- ....
- ....
- ....
- ....

STEPS

- ....
- ....
- ....
- ....
- ....
- ....

Printed in Great Britain
by Amazon

72128147R00032